www.finishinglinepress.com

.

Heidegger Looks at the Moon

89 poems by

R. W. Haynes

Finishing Line Press
Georgetown, Kentucky

Heidegger Looks at the Moon

Publisher: Leah Huete de Maines
Editor: Christen Kincaid
Cover Art: R. W. Haynes
Author Photo: Ruth Hernández Haynes
Cover Design: Elizabeth Maines McCleavy

Order online: www.finishinglinepress.com
also available on amazon.com

Author inquiries and mail orders:
Finishing Line Press
P. O. Box 1626
Georgetown, Kentucky 40324
U. S. A.

Table of Contents

For my wife.

1]
The Border Balance Betrayal

She wanted to escape poetry and redeem
The poetic process and its errant course
Through misplaced hopes and monuments that seem
To disappear when struck by sunshine's force,
And now this elegy on the fiddle scrapes
(Unnervingly, if people had such nerves)
As her wasting spirit slowly escapes
And no residual remnant stays and serves.
She should have stayed in that other poem where
Wallace Stevens told us time stayed still
As it ground to cinders everything else there
But dying orange scent and faded will,
So might her spirit still be energized,
Or, faltering, be slightly less surprised.
His fanatical grip upon his ghost
Proves impoverishment in ghost and mind,
And when he needs good sustenance the most
A ghost of cold regret is all he'll find.
Most committees suck, and when one's soul
Is no more than a meeting of cold-eyed thieves,
Dividing profits from corners they control,
And it adjourns, the vacuum it leaves
Out-sucks all others, and he then may see
His gifts were wasted, his useless property
An evil dream, his life of falsity,
Briefly before him, the last lucidity,
As justice draws him downward, finally.

2]
Meditation in a Mild Hurricane: As *Dolly* Approaches
Laredo before Sunrise

Our meteorologists coolly pronounce
This an interaction of heat and cold, wet
And dry, atmospheric pressure that mounts
And subsides toward a median state, yet
These philosophers find themselves compelled
To talk of personal traits in this rotation
Of winds and clouds and moisture all impelled
By laws of science clear in explanation.
A poet should agree with the scientists here
For his science and theirs achieves a unity
As more than ever meets the eye can appear
Intuitive to all, as any fool can see.
Aristotle's pleasure and harmony
Thus plays well with meteorology.

Aristotle argued that pain is agitation
Of the integral soul's natural harmony
And that sweet pleasure is the restoration
Of that harmonious integrity.
This storm, like some response to urgent prayer
By Shelley, or Elijah, sweeps the plains,
Scattering the salvation of moisture there
With the remorseless justice of its rains,
And brings to mind, as it always does for me,
The essence of drama, not imitation,
As Aristotle argued—complacently,
Perhaps—but the embodiment of creation.
We are the storms, Hedda Gabler and Lear
And Oedipus, blasted ashore right here.

And those cascades of blessed condensation
Bring a sympathetic synthesis
Between urgencies of our situation
And whatever you wish to designate this
Readiness to listen and to wait for rain
Washing down the dust from the mesquite

And cactus of this hostile Texas plain,
Watering and cooling down this land of heat,
A meditative, patient thoughtfulness
Harmonious with the motions of the storm,
Aware the drama is solutionless
And has for us no Aristotelian form.
This whirling theater of enormous forces
Skirts madly past, scattering our resources.

3]
To the Disenchanted Forest

If we doubt that this pinto-bean moon
Is actually spherical, or that the oblique
Emotions in orbit, jokes from a buffoon,
Reflect a coherence too tedious to seek,
If we, in short, view academically
The grasping process of expedience
And justify epistemologically
Recreant honor and defaulted sense,
We've simply vanished into the wandering wood
Of empty spirit, gone at last into
The dark place we once feared, gone for good
Under the mindless tyranny we knew
Lethargy and greed must generate,
The wilderness of hopeless, exhausted hate.

4]
Departing Tennessee

Without pursuing transient irritations
Or focusing too madly on the middle course,
Congratulating one's image's moderations,
Or forcibly enforcing abstinence from force,
With gracefully reluctant recognition,
Restless peace as knavish knives come out,
Mindless pride disdaining inanition
And the idealism cynics prate about,
I see no better way to do good things
Than this cloud of chaotic thought permits,
For the darker choices I know madness brings
Erupt in either paralysis or fits.
Silence is best when these spirits attack,
If cross-wrought figures fail to drive them back.

Every day is Halloween, if you let it be,
And with this festive, poetic approach,
Formulas are funny masks and validity
A fine, fat pumpkin become a golden coach.
Too much respect is poison: complacency
Surrenders quickly to friendly-seeming eyes
Reinforced convincingly by flattering lies,
Steady and deadly, and then, finally,
Conceit annihilates itself again,
Vulnerability, never long unattended
By hungry predators ready to move in,
Helpless, as usual, and unfriended
In the messy necessity usually caused
When the natural check on vanity has paused.

On this day I perceive, with some clarity,
The force of benevolence, familiarity
Unscolded by selfishness, generosity
Of spirit somehow somewhat strange to me.
The quiet words that come with a Spartan tone
Convey an exotic hospitality
And the sense as well that when they are gone

Their generous force may well abide with me.
I've heard Gadamer speak mysteriously
Of Wallace Stevens' jar in Tennessee,
A Modernist image embodying poetry:
Today that jar is at least half full for me.
Ready for the sky, I gather my few things
For flight, braced for what tomorrow brings.

5]
Facebook Teiresias

I will eventually appear to be
A somewhat better bargain as a friend,
But disguise is my abhorrence, generally,
And there is, nor will be, nothing to defend,
As those with eyes to see must decide
Where their investments will best be placed
And then enjoy what profits are supplied
As life develops, new expense is faced.
The old man will remain as he remained,
Unembittered, perhaps somewhat relieved,
Not to have owned, operated or maintained
The lively prospects in which you believed.
Not having changed, he constitutes no threat
To upset economy, generate debt.

6]
Barking and Sparking

Dogs do play politics, but their machinations
Laughably proclaim their devious conniving
More transparent than the representations
We think necessary for surviving.
Applying, though, proportionality,
Envisioning an abler evaluation
Viewing us likewise, does our acuity
Do us more credit than the canine situation?
Cerberus! Are two heads better than one
When both are empty? Are all fools the same
When all is finally said, or barked, and done
And final justice weighs our praise and blame?
Is the difference between eloquence and barking
A mere matter of a few more neurons sparking?

7]
Glad to Be a Stranger

It is good to be a stranger where society
Reflects like twisted mirrors the solipsistic
Projections of emptiness, grinning foolishly,
Mentally overpowered by the simplistic,
Empowered by gadgets and electricity,
Delighted by dim superficiality.
The lotus-eaters' half-stoned colloquy
Achieves at best a specious affectation
Sustaining complacent juvenility
Inflated greatly by bogus education,
So nothing should make anyone want to be
More familiar in this situation:
Regret is best where mindlessness prevails
And humanity overwhelmingly fails.

8]
Old Sol's Paint Shop

The sun shows us the marvels everywhere
And with its light can paint on poverty
A patience, on ruin a wisdom so that there
We find understanding suddenly.
Its absence, too, functions to defend
The urgency of light, the much-deplored
Absence of a benevolent friend
Whose kind advice keeps all in accord.
Sleeplessness itself seeks its end
When the light of the mind, craving connection
With the eye of day, endeavors to pretend
Dawn has arrived from a different direction.
Then sleep comes with light, a stimulating rest
Stolen as the sun steals, smiling, west.

9]
Black Friday in the Texas Thrift Store

The man with the outraged voice
Gripped a black plastic clock
Shaped like a modernist pretzel.
It looked like it had been found behind
A burnt-out garage, after too much time.
"The price is too high," he complained.
"And the time is wrong," I replied,
With more sympathy than intended.
"No, no," he said, "the time is fine.
All it needs is batteries to work.
But just look at the shape of it:
I think it's perfect for time, don't you?"
"Um, yas," I philosophized slowly,
"I see what you mean. Time and pretzels,
You're quite right. But do you think it works?"
He glanced sharply at me. "Of course it works.
The shape is right, the time is right,
It's just the price that's wrong."
"But everything's half off today," I tried,
Not that the honor of the Texas Thrift Store
Mattered greatly to me, but time still does.
"It doesn't matter, does it?" he complained.
"The time is fine, but still the price is wrong."

10]
Another Meeting

We academic wizards draw our designs,
To the hilarity of devils everywhere,
Abracadabras, pentagrams and lines
Of mystical figures which magically bear
Powers of a realm either dim or dark,
To appropriate credit among our fellow thieves,
To settle scores, get rich, make our mark
In meaninglessness piling up like leaves.
Here and there, however, a merry light
Plays upon some spirit, free of the blight
Of sordid association, whose rhythm is right
And whose gracious motion is a promising sight:
A radiant planet smiling on a stormy night,
Launching hope of hope in a hopeless fight.

11]
The Name of My Muse

I do not know the name of my Muse
Or how her inspiration regulates
The flow of words I slowly grope to choose
As her half-heard, half-dreamed voice dictates.
In some organic, comprehensive way,
All my engagements link intimately
As ancient illuminations fitfully play
Between revelation and history.
This benign force of imagination
Sustains the consciousness of reverence,
Endowing both perception and vocation
With hope of wisdom and some competence.
No name is needed for this intimacy
That both awakens and determines me.

12]
Cicero Fumes against Cleopatra

We do not need another queen in Rome.
While we do revere the wisest Greeks,
In Cleopatra, Plato hardly speaks:
Caesar would be wiser to send her home.
Egypt! O when Plato studied there
And tuned *philosophia* to the spheres
He never thought that in the cycling years
We'd have in Italy a Sphinx to bear.
O Caesar, moderate thy lust apace,
Remembering all thy scribbled tragedies,
Lest this Medea, crazed by jealousies,
Decimate the children of our race.
Old Oedipus, who saved Thebes from a curse,
Would pity our Rome, whose Sphinx is even worse.

13]
Small Sips for the Old

In what's left of that vitality
Focused once on balancing a vision
Of perfect catharsis simultaneously
Identifying an unfortunate decision,
And in the stupor halfway felt between
Encroaching lethargy and distant star,
This pulled-apartness, drowsily keen,
Acutely dull, tentatively gone too far,
Renders ancient and amber my whisper now,
And I don't want to hear how anyone feels,
As Dr. Bradford used to shrug and say;
Killers kill, liars lie, time steals.
Like old whiskey, old wisdom tastes best,
Small sips for the old make for better rest.

14]
For Gretchen

Quiet lights flickering faintly proclaim
Unspeakable destruction unspeakably far
From our tragedies. They raged before we came
For ages, and ages from now each raging star
Will burn down to nothing and then expire
Unremembered in the kind of apathy
We attribute to nature's physical empire,
Stars ourselves, of interiority.
But if a child passes from our vision
Our hearts adamantly demand to know
The reason; agony and indecision
And helplessness combine at once to throw
The rational aside and with urgent force
Seek consolation from the most perfect source.

15]
Drama Critic Dismasted by *Gone with the Wind*

I have discovered for myself one useful thing in life, which is to judge the
people we know as if they were dead….
  —Stark Young, *The Pavilion*

Well, perhaps I was just born to paint
And expatiate upon what dramatists do,
And not compete with Hollywood's flashy crew,
And lick my wounds and weep, and nearly faint.
In eighteen sixty-two, my father went
To serve with Forrest in that losing fight,
A teen-aged boy who thought the cause was right,
Who thought he knew what honor really meant.
And I, today, salute his kindly ghost,
His honor, marksmanship, and attitude,
Though now the Stars and Bars have rudely screwed
One not arriving first with the most.
Blasted by Margaret's mighty grand slam,
Frankly, my dear, I do now give a damn.

16]
Beauty's Tyranny, Reason's Hot Dialogue

Never begin a poem so aggressively
That it makes a foolish editor lose his mind.
Unless, that is, you write for someone free,
Less frivolous and shallow, not quite so blind,
A partner in this quixotic fuck-up fest
Browsing happy madness where the buzzards rest,
And the lost graves hum with secrecy
And the storms sing out the slaves have liberty
And love explains it always does its best.
No, you never begin like that, with two
Left feet, leaky britches with a seasoned shine,
An empty grin that don't know what to do
But hold its shabby, weathered cardboard sign
That says: "It's mine; it's mine.
"Ha ha, it's mine—everything is mine."

17]
We Wade through Unseen Fogs

We wade through fogs of demonic mist
Even in sunlight, even when the clear sun
Declares toxicity not even to exist;
Even then, gassed, perception is undone.
Poisoned nerves attempt regeneration
As the attacks fitfully subside
And learn a sufficient respiration
Where the natural course of life was denied.
After all, though, the sun's declaration
May as well pass as the last word on this:
Practical wisdom is practical salvation,
And too much knowledge is not much to miss.
So, cheap *diablitos*, this deliberate error
Scrubs and erases all your toxic terror.

18]
Valediction from the Train West

My part of the death train chugged on past
Your bright resort some time ago, and someone
Threw a bottle at it just for fun,
For fun does entertain, but does not last,
And its empty bottles, the hilarity
Of senescent fools' ominous forecast
That stupid exuberance evaporates fast,
Gather, with the miles, ponderous gravity,
And the dark tunnel which concludes the run
Welcomes the mind to its opacity,
Saluting this last desperate dignity,
And this last departure from the sun.
We've left some silently, waved to the rest,
Relieved to leave, finally rolling west.

19]
A Plain Plate of Beans and Rice

Beans and rice are good enough at last,
And in the absence of articulated light
This Stoic thought is pleasing at first sight,
Generating images where ideas are cast,
And juggling old forgiveness like a ball
Torn from strange hands in a scorpion's pit
To play with here and muse upon it,
While old things slide and cool shadows fall.
Yes, the answer is still a simple no,
For ornament has a proper place elsewhere
And this here and now are never there,
And I just let the lights and shadows grow
And go, and need no wise complexity
To keep time hog-tied temporarily.

20]
A Little Ham for the Kaiser

"I shook with dread lest the wolves might eat Napoleon."
—Stark Young

We must tolerate some tyrants. Human years
Of helplessness cultivate our fears
And train us in groveling routines
Which pacify the giants looming above
And make us skilled pretenders of love
And calculating little schemers of scenes.
Fast-learning kids, we dodge the bully's wrath;
Minnows in the shallows, we brightly flee
Deep-water monsters roving randomly,
Darting reflexively from the dangerous path,
Arriving at last to our designated state
Of dignity, we look about us to see
Whose egos must be treasured diligently,
For this is the service we negotiate.

Yet in such servitude grows a desire
To see the autocrat's complacency
Give way to recognition, a peripety
Hurling vain pettiness into dreadful fire,
And pain from what one now contemplates
Is partly purged as that vast wheel rotates.

21]
The Wobbly Pendulum Threatens to Strike

The pendulum roughly marks the phases
Of the domination of brutality,
When the mind twists unnaturally
To savagery, the envious eye gazes
Hungrily at others' prosperity,
And bitter greed drives the fools it crazes.
So now that villain over there may not
Wear a Nazi uniform or salute
A maniac as master, but surely he's got
The vicious attitude that would suit
A goose-stepping idiot from Hitler's men,
And his good Frau, whose crazy face would stare
The paint off a Russian tank, deserves to win
An Iron Cross to decorate her hair.

The nurse of philosophy, external disdain,
Washes off accretions of pretentious grime
The impulse of ignorance acquires over time
And clears away shame with its clarifying rain.
Its cousin Experience may silently approve
This process, but don't trust her shifty eyes:
Experience tells you experience sometimes lies
Just to feed itself and make things move.
So welcome here, O contemptuous sneer,
Fast-averted eye and painful grin,
For here comes mortal leprosy again,
Dragging a contagious poverty near.
Is repetition lightning and thunder, too?
Will you forget how this small storm rolled through?

22]
Flexing for Restraint

You did not need to pile explanations
On explanations you might have made
With a lift of the hands, a twist of the blade,
Echoing earlier conversations.
But then you must have suddenly understood—
For it was too quiet, as men of action declare
In ancient films, danger sensed somewhere—
That stressing the script did no one any good.
Oh, blessed restraint, that rarely if ever arrives
To feast us on silence, our only protection
From brutal madness, throw your quiet correction
Like a vast, forgetful blanket, covering our lives.
For here, struggling to control this strife,
We half-grasp slick wisdom half-learned from life.

23]
Last Half of a Heartfelt Dialogue

Intensity? Here? In this smudge of ink?
Where silence resonates down the gloomy halls
And twitches misery's cobwebs on the walls,
Here? Which eye cares, madam, do you think?
But in a while the desert sun will rise
And desert critters will try their morning voices
In a choir that lustily rejoices
As strong sunlight feasts its shining eyes.
Now, you will have intensity then,
And memory of this will fade for good
Back into ancient poetry's dark wood
As blessed sunlight lights the world again.
Can we make patience, a haven in night fear,
Pull itself slowly together right here?

24]
Hawk in the Mist

That's what thought should always be like,
Gliding with dignity, unthought intent,
Like part of the wind itself, its weightless ascent
Actualizing like good, well-sworn words.

Above cold forest and steaming fjord,
An unheard heartbeat keeping perfect time declares
Mysterious mastery of shifting airs,
Swooping to conclude in covering cloud.

25]
Attending a Light, Freezing Fog

We wanted to go back to Oslo. That worked out
For Ibsen, *mas o menos*, who reconnected
Inner fogs with those he recollected
And which coldly welcomed him, no doubt.
But we got over that, for golden Mexico,
Golden, bloody Mexico—a dream
In which mad murderers laugh and scream
In the dramatic center of the zero,
Parrots and papayas explode and sing,
And incomparable ladies with matchless eyes
Calculate our witless calculus of lies—
Golden Mexico, *ay!* drives everything
Into chastening subordination
Before its violent imagination.

So scratch off that hope of a devastating stroll
Down for a schnapps in the Grand Café,
Tequila has blown that cold schnapps away,
And though we revere that side-whiskered troll,
My ghosts speak Spanish and love a good joke
Almost as much as life, since angels stand
Smiling and kindly cooperative at hand,
For we all must go up, even if in smoke.
Ibsen's war against mortality
Ennobled art, but can an avalanche
Provide satisfaction back at the ranch?
Is there no more fashionable way of being free?
Can a stronger case mystically be made
For the magic mariachi serenade?

The storm was dying as we said goodbye
To good things, farewells, in a kind of frantic
False rejection of the gestural romantic,
Scrolling hungrily for the satisfying lie.
And clouds threw open their glowing gates
As perfect light cascaded everywhere,
Supercharging drama perceived in empty air,

The moment *known* as it evaporates.
Right. We should be glad it slipped away
So elegantly, with such unnoticed grace
No one perceived how each dramatic face
Crumbled to nothing: no need then to say
How that play augmented human history,
And if I murmur now, don't listen to me.

Our theater speaks in unspeakable ways.
We grapple with that concreteness
Necessary for an aesthetic completeness,
Yet each hopeful curtain that we raise,
Drawing the future upon our childish hearts,
Reaching where the dream of happiness starts,
Returns our past on us unsought and cold,
A strange and lingering bargain, startling but old.

26]
Ominous Sounds from the Getty Hexameters

Who can doubt that healing powers
Wait in the shadows, pondering
Intervention in our hapless wandering
Toward whatever peripety is ours?
Does one pray beseechingly to these,
Or is that fatal? Is there only grace
Kindly awarded to the averted face?
Is recovery better than disease?
Get the rooster feathers, the sacred knife,
And the gaudy gourds so we can rattle
As if anemic Death's afraid of battle
And hides his face to save his bony life,
And we'll secure this poetic prescription,
Chanting lucky curses from the Egyptian.

27]
Cold Water Wisdom Up North

Surely one approves of deep, cold fjords
Demonized by time, imagination,
And icy paralysis of volatile sensation,
Beckoning violence to Viking lords,
But in warm parlors, soft musical sound
Strokes and teases, pulls stealthy comfort around,
Seduces history into a drowsy sleep
In which the mind's unforgiving blade
Buries itself, old true steel betrayed,
In hot marshmallows forty fathoms deep.
Yet, through this soporific haze, at last,
A troubling sound of a shrewd brass alarm
Disturbs this rest, and signals dreadful harm
At hand, approaching both fatal and fast.
The volume of cold trouble forces out
A cry, as one looks frantically about.

28]
Colonel Sanders Needs Love, Too

The hero crows, the heroine clucks back,
Both featherheads in chicken-yard roles,
Mad as wet poultry, wing-flapping souls
In dramatic ecstasies, their yackety-yak
Besieges the heavens with an eloquence
Betokening nature's rich intensity
Of wit and color, symphonic cacophony,
Providence exploding inside the backyard fence.
And as those echoes blast forth distraction,
Other dramas wrap us in their charms,
Like friendly octopi with too many arms,
Involving our minds with too much interaction.
So we, like tenacious, outraged little birds,
Dodge through a storm of deciduous words.

29]
A Gusty Substance in Regret

Circumstantial patterns for emulation
Invite a formal turn around the floor
For a gesture of consideration,
And then, if nothing flies, out the door,
To the litany of endless fragmentation,

And wet sand holds our urgent words no more
Before this light-headed resignation
That such convenient wisdom holds in store.

The sea hawk plunges madly for his prey,
His mate intent to see his accuracy,
Dodging, hovering and soaring, fiercely they play,
Matching in manners, raucous in courtesy:
Cries mean more than words out at sea,
In the sky's own light, flying recklessly.

Dizzy is a fair term for any state
Not held as hostage by a frightening force
But disengaged, if briefly, to levitate
Where thrilling visions bubble up and course,

Holding off the grinning fangs which show
The truest love of all the love we know,
Eluding warnings always flashed too late,
To moderate the force of the finishing blow.

Dizzy it is, but, as gravity climbs
The landscape, we revoke negotiation
Not formulated in starlight and rhymes
Shaping a curve of waking consecration,
Locking out both death and gravitation,
Delirious with delightful incantation.

30]
Jack Ruby's Smoked Ribs Recipe

Oh, hell, forget it. You can't think about
Thirty things at once. Cooking, to be good
Requires peace of mind and seasoned wood
And all distractions barricaded out.
No girls, no cops, no guns, just mental liberty
And savory smoke, and time, no shocks.
If I glide thoughtlessly through wrecks and rocks,
A sceptral fork to wield authority,
Nothing can touch my all-explosive nerve:
Nothing will torment me to draw and fire
Or stoke this bed of hot coals higher.
I stand in my black apron, poised to serve.
My kingdom is my backyard under the sun.
I stand contented when these ribs are done.

31]
Balaam's Burrito on the Act of Treason

Listen, Judas, we all make bad mistakes,
But betrayal aforethought of a loving friend
Deserves notoriety and a fitting end,
And, though your problems are your own heartaches,
Ugly actions are inevitably shared,
And, even as friendship evaporates,
Regret obscures itself but quietly waits,
While a mist of penitence congregates
Where the execution is prepared.
Better if honesty, silverless, had dared
To state its case before the greedy mind
And chosen love, left appetite behind.
Philosophy comes in handy where trap doors wait
For the unphilosophic to procrastinate.

32]
Rats of the Normal School: The Pledge of Allegiance

Driven not only by squealing data but by
The hounds of pusillanimity racing
Us, the sold-out rats berserkly chasing
Vanishing rewards, we try and try
To grab, escape, tear loose, assimilate
Vertiginous, indigestible feasts;
And, swarming like demented beasts
Around a fallen, bleeding litter-mate,
Show professional designs upon success.
After all, the protocol is devotion
To running in place with maximum motion,
Achieving maximum meaninglessness.
Get out of my way, sister or brother;
I'll throw you down as I would another.

33]
When Light is Short on the Stratford Stage

Predation and reluctance tend to contend,
As do many better things, contention
Posing appetite's reflex to defend
Its lust against hesitant abstention.
Let me be more precise, because I see
Your attention fading, your bloodshot eye
Searching for merciful escape from me
And the tedious words which I live by.
Where was I? All right, then, what I mean
Is that a coward dies a thousand times—
No. Hell, no. The spirit that I have seen...
May be the devil of forgotten crimes,
And my reluctant impulse, I allow,
May have become cruel predation now.

34]
The Swarm

Old words keep some kinds of resonance
When breathed, yet on the page they show
A coolness and an insincerity
Which dry up drama, let the steam escape
From warm expression, draw the judging eye
Of the critic or call for disdain.

So this is a spell for mandolin and harp,
For just-contained jealousy and spite,
For confidences and for bloody threats
Whispered outside taverns in starlight.

If you step up and turn your head a bit
To hear, your eyes alight to learn my news
Of dangers and delights and hidden traps,
I will assure you, though my words be old,
My voice is haunted through and through by songs
Beaten in breasts through torment and hope,
Chorused in kitchen and down country roads,
Alive as your eyes to our destinies,
Resonating like a tense swarm of bees.

35]
The Slayer of Pain

A few days ago, we went to war,
And now the flying beagle of peace extends
His colored ears over the blessed earth,
Giving thanks for the blessed bones of peace.

And bless you, too, Great Hush Puppy,
Anaesthetic flying object full of bones,
Peacemaker, inspiration, damn good dog,
Whose eyes defeat all malice everywhere.

And now the war is gone, and we review
The smoking ruins of history, yes, mm-hmm,
Breakfast in bed, green jays outside yodeling
Like rednecks, love everywhere, music etc.

Until the clouds of truth roll in again
And we need you, super hero,
Flying above.

36]
The Other Delphic Teaching

I confess! Counterclockwise went
That whole buffet of delicious crap
With one yo-ho, one colossal slap,
Bingo! Out went all Good Fortune sent.
Staring at the smoking shards around,
With bits of salmon sticking in my beard,
As little mocking cherubs laughed and jeered
At Goliath, shocked and half-dead on the ground.
Yep, that's it, fellows, I've half died,
Reaching for the rafters, mad and blind,
And here comes Nemesis. She'll remind
Us of the deadly penalty of pride.
Ha. Her news is emptiness to me:
A circle completed everyone can see.

37]
On the Flight from Embarrassment

"As I recall,
It was late November,
When Lord Byron tripped
Upon his virile member."
—Leo Rascón

Humiliation, the donkey that walks
Us toward our blessedest destination,
Overhears the man who foolishly talks
And crushes him to silent meditation.
Pride and anger serve this patient critic well
And loose-lipped instinct blabs his fatal name.
Give his quiet dignity reverence, or foretell
Agony of bitter regret, remorseful shame.
Count your steps in peace, find a careful way
To do your work thoughtfully, show respect,
To be a modest soldier, watching every day
To maintain humility, not lose track or neglect.
Humiliation still will locate you soon
And light you up like the harvest moon.

I shouldn't have broken at the first attack.
Excuses are for those who have a claim
To better virtue and can fall back
On good intentions without bitter blame.
But I put my foot in it, thoughtless, I gave
The store away, sold out to the thieves,
Ran for cover though I once was brave,
And earned the shame a smirking rat receives.
What now? Inside my heavy hanging head
Flies buzz aloud, whining mockingly.
How can I now be justly comforted
With penitential mind, remorsefully?
Surrender can sometimes seem clearly right,
But cowards feel its lasting, poisoned bite.

38]
The Fond Farewell

You dying sycophants of life's flirtation,
I leave you without furious expression,
Venomous thought, or bitter condemnation.
I'd say we're alike enough, a likely confession
To be disbelieved, I'd like to believe,
So let my farewell, empty of disdain
For any, serve all a happy lack of pain,
A gleaming platter of nothing to retrieve.
We warm and cool ourselves with projections
As imagination innocently plays
Till we achieve our quota of rejections
And check out quietly to end our days.
I lift my hand to you as darkness falls,
A gesture unseen, as better business calls.

39]
The Wrong End of I-35

A Poem for Bob Dylan

I asked the writing teacher who can't write
To write me a reference to eternal doom
And send it to the living from the tomb,
But she just waved her checkbook in the light
And laughed, and ran toward the evil sea
Where bloody-beaked gulls swarm ferociously.
I turned then to the man in beard and cloak,
Holding a bowl, and asked him to explain
Why wisdom leaks away like dirty rain,
And he asked me, "Is this some kind of joke?
Don't you know that real philosophy
Didn't begin until my mother had me?"
Elusive answers? Yet these do suffice,
For explanations melt down here like ice.

40]
The Best Tlacoyos in Chickasawhatchee

> Back before he was extinct, I mean, of course,
> The Great Common-Sense Woodpecker, bless his heart,
> You could sit here on the porch, sober as a judge,
> And watch pterodactyls chasing the bugs
> Back and forth around the glowing moon.

Back then, that is, before it all went to hell,
That boy from Bacon County, what was his name?
His daddy drove a log truck, it finally caught fire
And burned down the Primitive Baptist Church,
But the pastor's German Shepherd barked in time,
And they saved the parsonage. I'll remember his name,
The boy's, not the German Shepherd's, here in a little,
But anyhow, he played the mandolin, not the dog,
Of course, but the kid from Bacon, pretty well,
And he'd park his butt on the steps and play old songs,
"Pretty Polly," "Darlin' Corey," and "Watch Out, Young Ladies,"
And Grandmama, who did watch out pretty well
When she was young, according to her, anyhow,
Would tap her foot as if arthritis was a song.

> And up in the sky, the constellations danced,
> And passenger pigeons flowed across forever,
> And old songs fused together like aqueducts
> Washing all the grief away that any of us ever had.

41]
Bloody Daggers

If huge clouds rise from incineration
Of good, if philosophy madly stares
As music drags into incarceration,
And imbeciles' vain cacophony blares
Where stirring strings and noble lilting flutes
Stroked the spirit, calmed the furious rage
Whose force such sound delicately refutes,
And sends it docile back into its cage—
If omens of disorder such as these
Disturb your peace of mind and sleep,
Add twisting pain to your anxieties,
Threatening hopes you always hoped to keep,
Then pray that fools learn wisdom, greedy thieves
Grow honest, bloody daggers in their sleeves.

42]
Train Coughing West

Hack, hack, departure, departure,
I don't mind if sanity slides
Right out of here and silently hides,
As it's outlived its usefulness.

We run out of stuff we don't need.
Being strong and sturdy, having cash,
And now, eyes open in the trash,
We greet satisfaction.

Go on out of here and tell
Folks down the line that soon
They'll hear the best part of the tune,
If they have ears to hear.

It pays to testify, young people,
And that mystery explains why
My hands are empty and my hopes high,
As I gaze at that shrinking light.

43]
Some Hope Whispers

Some hope whispers as the line of text
Creeps toward its fate, and what happens next—
When the sleeping dog wakes and shakes his ears,
And drowsy dreams, exhausted owls, glide back
Into unchanted forests, and hide, and pray
Rest and darkness will erase their fears—
Depends on what these hieroglyphs lack,
Years of rest and darkness smoothly slip away,
And when the garbage slides into the Styx,
Little it matters who did the best tricks.
Distant flutes and clarinets sing
With faint, seductive harmony,
But a dry rattle, nearer, ominously,
Drags back old prudence in everything.

44]
Minor Demons, Minor Angels

Minor demons have their favorite places:
Linguistics books, acceptances,
Administrative grins and table dances,
Juvenile ideas, and angled staircases.

Minor angels, though some care is due
Their upward mobility, hang around
Cooking smells, plows breaking ground,
Brave proposals where new love is true:
They love to hover kindly next to these,
And with their friends, the honey-gathering bees.

45]
Echo in Leaves

Green shades once conveyed an association
Someone was organically swayed to employ
To show the force of nature's proliferation
And the shocked mind's desperate need to enjoy
Restorative rest and quiet contemplation.
Thus appetite, calmed by natural harmony
And by the sweetness of anticipation,
Kindly lends vigor to starved philosophy.
O poet's ghost, this reverent invocation
Braids your concerns and mine like living vines,
If I may say so to one of your station,
And some reluctant bitterness in your lines
Finds some sympathy in my situation.
The fruit stand is closed, no peaceful promenades
Are scheduled, nothing behind those green shades.

46]
Lost Grave: Buzzards' Roost Cemetery, Goliad County

For Eliza Holliday Horton

We don't ask too much from friendship, my friend,
Or kinship, either, for these abandoned graves
Have joined together with those of your slaves,
Lost, found, a temporary end
To labor and trouble. Let's rest beneath these skies,
Our monuments murmurs of kind consolation,
Our hopes gone to seed, disintegration
Putting things ready for a bright sunrise.
No more massacres, except where bees
Massacre indolence, loud happy birds
Slaughter the silence with rude-squawked words
Among lost graves now hidden by trees.
Are you there, Eliza? We've come a long way
From old Alabama, wouldn't you say?

47]
Those Cowboy Thrillers

If we were racing ponies to the saloon
Or roping mavericks out in the thorny brush,
Figurative mariachis blasting a tune,
Blood pressure raging in exuberant rush,
Credits rolling, wise smiles all around,
With the bad guys finally stuck underground,
Why, that would lift our drab situation
Stampeding a juicier imagination.
Right. And then the depredation
Of gnawing success, a stealthy nutrient
Eroding mortal complacency to drive
Life to the desperation lack of action sent…
Well, tell me, will that keep us alive?
Will those cowboy thrillers help us survive?

48]
Big Jake's Cowboy Breakfast

Out here we like our ladies cute,
Our politicians stupid, our legal code
Tailored to profit and to pollute.
Comfort and Damascus are on the same road,
And all the white folks except Democrats
Are headed for Jerusalem to receive,
Grinning greasily like shit-eating rats,
Diplomas in bullshit for what they believe.
The profit of the rugged individual
Requires that the rugged fill his belly
Regardless if widows and orphans have theirs full,
So teaches Texas, and Machiavelli.
Go whine in Oklahoma if you want to cry,
But not in Ft. Stockton. Root, hog, or die!

49]
Downtown Waco. Midnight. Heidegger Looks at the Moon.

The Bush Library really should be here,
For each dead city needs a laugh or two,
A little something so the skeletons can jeer
On nights like this when there's little to do
And nothing to haunt but the haunting lack of hope
Where words are born to sputter anxiously
Toward brief life in some half-bungled trope
Irrecoverable etymologically.
Is there another cyclone on its way
To re-mix this desperation here?
To make words and deeds mutually obey
A dim correspondence—never more clear
Than the misshapen moon cruising so high
Over the Brazos in the hopeless Waco sky?

50]
Reverent Caution

Is the alignment of our obedience
Unperverted by false appetite?
And does our gently-nourished reverence
Draw a proper power, true insight?
We see the ineffectual theories
Of pompous blowhards bring ridicule,
Making others view us as they please
As helpless hybrids between rogue and fool.
Do we survive to placate envious greed
And calm with lying words the frantic minds
Of masquerading scoundrels? Surely we need
A greater satisfaction as life unwinds,
But to be forceful is so often unwise
That reverent caution stares down our eyes.

51]
The Owl Soliloquizes a Ghostly Good-Bye

The owl of wisdom wakes as sunlight dies,
And, as the forest fades to ghostliness,
Confidence yields as the light grows less,
And the bird of darkness eerily cries.
And now the stars show truth unto the wise,
Who know the rarity of commonness,
The secret perfection of invisible process
Of the devoted algebra that shapes the skies.
And, as I think of ghosts who came to me
In brighter times, drawn by mad attraction
Set mysteriously into careless action,
Kind darkness hides a crushing sympathy,
And comfort quibbles now that wisdom lies,
And that some quiet kinship never dies.

52]
Colonel Klink Comes to Himself on the Russian Front

Death and I have become warrior friends.
The cold preserves our eye-to-eye regard
As we quip tersely about mortality's ends
And smile at notions life and death are hard.
The other stuff is gone: anxiety,
Reputation, pretense, self-respect
Evaporate as courage comes to me
Like merciless truth, sudden and direct.
Our *Donner und Blitzen* are a pathetic show
Of impotent force delusive to the obsessed,
And imperial dreams just callow bravado
Annihilated by this reversed conquest.
The cannon toll goodbye, this emptiness lost:
Collapse, detonation, the blistering rage of frost.

53]
To a Raving Romantic

So emotions, being natural, must exceed
In cogency, immediacy, and force
The quieter powers that regulate the need
For departures from the conscientious course.
And their demands, so forcibly expressed,
Justify most of the damage they do,
Since, children of nature, we function best
Convulsed in response to the beautiful and true.
Keenly attuned to the raging ocean's mystery,
We must stand liberated from all restraint,
Including that of wisdom and of history,
And penetrate realms not meant for the faint.
So goes the story. Other stories tell
A scientific trainwreck does as well.

54]
This Day's Recognition

Wherever the eye falls, perceived potential
Awaits a gracious consideration,
And this day, delineated here by the sun,
Enlightens memory, clarifies the essential.
The truth rises daily but it descends
Only in that our limitations
Prevent cosmic circumnavigations,
And when it seems illumination ends,
We rest a bit then in the quiet shade
Till the planet adjusts itself appropriately
And the light of dawn, awaited faithfully,
Greets quiet insight inwardly conveyed.
Reverence provokes a gentle ambition
To have each day this day's recognition.

55]
The Sophist Counts His Chickens

It's not so much whether one lies as when
And how much. The truth is often unclear
And changes its appearance now and then.
And we speak words we are surprised to hear
Though we endeavored to speak reasonably,
Gambling on good intentions to harmonize,
Not to deceive but to locate the frequency
Where harmonious benevolence lies.
Thus exculpated, pushing the thought aside
That intentions are no better than the mind,
One wanders into the falsehood just denied,
Blindly relying on precepts left behind.
If these evolutions occur naturally,
How can I, really, object to falsity?

56]
Stevens the Insurance Man

An indistinct point in the evaluation
Of the quality of quality is the unmarked place
Where this over-refined estimation,
Conceived in good intention, incurs the disgrace
Of nonsensicality, and then
What value it might have accumulated
Empties itself back out again,
And the gathering harmony is dissipated.
Although you married the girl upon the dime
And duked it out down in the Sunshine State
With Hemingway, both loaded at the time,
Abstraction tempted you to abdicate
The highest inspiration of your art,
Withstanding which was the policy of your heart.

57]
And Furthermore

Then comes the time, who lives to see't
That going shall be used with feet.
The Fool

You control, to some extent, your energy
And whether it flows to negotiate fear
Or to seek a sweet, symphonic quality
Of active understanding, honest, sincere,
And simple, but visionary and insightful.
And though anxiety never goes away
For long, it will return to you less frightful
If you have taught yourself to obey
Your Muses, to find the course of action,
Or hesitation, harmonious for you
Philosophically, a satisfaction
And a strategic sustenance, too.
Wisely choose wisdom, then, is my advice:
So would I have, if I could have chosen twice.

58]
Life Is Like the Tex-Mex Railroad

Some of the varieties of loss sit well
With the balance of consciousness, and some
Threaten the perception of the parallel
Tracks of existence, the equilibrium
Approximated in the course of this track
Between good and evil as the cat's tail wags
And what we have lost, or can't give back,
Weighs more ponderously, and the burden drags.
Derangement diminishes appreciation,
Revulsion approaches a critical mass,
But alleviating loss affords quiet liberation
And the burdensome grief manages to pass.
And the fading light of the vanishing caboose
Is blessed release as the dream is cut loose.

59]
Upon This Rock

"the suggested anguish of falling"
—Maud Bodkin

Everyone's an architect, but no foundations
Underlie their clever, cutting-edge erections,
Specious, meretricious creations
Aimed at comfortable currency collections.
Nightmares issue from these fantasy realms
Of baseless, vertiginous otiosity;
A cheap hell inevitably overwhelms
The author of smirking superficiality.
It's difficult to build on solid stone,
But, as the third little piggy did,
I build a structure that will stand alone
Sheltering the precious content I have hid.
Youth seeks nightmares, but no more for me
Will rise that superfluous, ghastly fantasy.

60]
Careful Care before Carelessness

Dismissing, clinically, a lunch so fine
And so substantial as that one
As though some amoeba went to dine
On unspeakable scraplets it happened upon
Makes the ebbing storm of consciousness
A flock of small *demonios* of dust,
Collapsing in fatigue, sick of the mess,
Disintegrating carelessly, gust by gust.
But I don't take you so very seriously
In such matters, for you and I talk always,
And you can freely say such things to me
As our familiar counterpoint re-plays
And we re-load experience and ingenuity,
And ourselves, conversationally.

61]
Regeneration of Love

The backslid Baptist read Gospel commands
On the telephone in the dying Jesuit's ear,
"Take no thought," he said, as the nurse's hands
Held the telephone so the old man could hear,
And then "Behold the fowls of the air,"
And his friend tried to reply to him then,
But at the end no word was there
Except the original, and it may have been
A thoughtful joke that the homeward priest
Thought to deliver to his student then
When that conversation ceased
And the winged silence of friendship spoke
Of the promised promise that neither broke.

62]

The Real Reality Games: Illusion, Delusion, Collusion, Confusion

If time's justice is not let alone
To work, we will not justly sympathize
With those who thought that this world was their own
And bought with vicious tricks a worthless prize.
It does not matter, either, if we see
The execution of this justice here;
For the fulfillment of vengeful fantasy,
Though gratifying, tends to interfere
With understanding, as does all success
In imbecilic games, buffoonery
Always, itself injustice, more or less,
And all too often more mere cruelty.
Take no thought, then, for the grinning apes,
Or whether or not their wickedness escapes.

63]
Short Hymn to Smugness

Formalizing informality,
We blithely go from there to designate
All things falsely with glib variety,
As though sacred truth were never too late.

Forgive a certain dirtiness of mind
In this: too much fresh dust has choked
My vocabulary, and all the words I find
Fit nowhere in the text invoked.

I'll contemplate the garden awhile until
The fit passes, and, if I return,
Truth may offer a compromise that will
Turn out less distasteful to learn.

These skirmishes are crawling things
Dragging up and down old, rusty strings.

64]
Listen Here, Cassandra

Sometimes an improvised ritual will do:
If rhythm and dignity are attended to,
The oyster can be your world, your universe,
And when the grackles yack and the vultures curse,
You'll hum like a hummingbird, leaving them behind,
Hacking in a cloud of metaphoric dust,
Melodies and sweetness governing your mind
With gentle passions of hungry wanderlust.
I hope you can see this. It's plain to me.
But no one quite knows what another will see
In this land of traps and hallucinations,
Poisonous attractions, broken operations,
Miraculous rescues, delirious sensations,
And moments when pelicans glide graciously.

Let's define iconoclasm as not going along
With committees of meatheads, congregations
Of lazy hypocrites, stupid proclamations
By righteous dimwits who are always wrong.
If we were pelicans, sure, I'd gladly dive
With all the rest for croakers in the waves
And never ask why that collusion saves
Our tribe of canny fliers to survive.
Or if we were rattlers, stuttering an alarm
As we coil in deadly dignity,
That savage force would gather naturally,
With malice toward none, no intended harm.
Don't tread on our nature. And forever prepare
The safety of sympathy when our kind is there.

65]
Poetry 101, First Quarter of the Moon

Begin here. I'm leaving a space.

All right, now, what do you do?
We have the cameras activated.

The space is in your timing,
Not mine, mind you.

So when your hieroglyphic squiggles
Stand up and wiggle,
OK, hmm…

I'm leaving you more space.

Next step: Embracing the Narrative,
I mean, Narrating the Embrace…
You have to write this in the dark
With a dollar flashlight & a pen with 07 on it,
Mr. (or Ms.) Bond…

And see my poem about
The Great Speckled Ivory-Bill.

And here is how we do it in the Poets' Club:

When the Little Elf Lady Saved the Dogs

(Notes from Moon-Crazed Nights, Found on the Bedside Table
of an Ancient Pharisee)

Once upon a time, then, the wind worked contrary,
And dogs could show their faces without shame.
But the moon went orange, and everything changed,
So dogs wear masks now, each January.

The old timer hollered at the speed freak and said,
"Run for the river, or the peach trees are dead!"

The doorhinge murmured quietly
Like her mother's voice.
Glory, hallelujah,
Let all the foolish pups rejoice.

66]
Somebody Run Them Chickens out of the Circles of Purgatory

Circles of interest, casually tangential
Or overlapping, perhaps overbold,
Nervously jitterbug, mindful of essential
Discretion, that necessity to withhold
Enough information to deserve respect,
Even if empty, with all the white space
(Negative capability to connect)
Gleaming forth both from page and face.
And that dance goes on; here, however,
The circle has been squared, my dancing shoes
Sent off to the Goodwill forever,
No more romantic than the match-box blues.
And what's to touch, now, and what's to see. . .
Don't bother, and I won't, no longer me.

67]
Do One for the Guys with Two Left Feet

For Etta James

> *"And yet, Razumov, …you have not the face of a lucky man."*
> —Sophia Antonovna

You know how it is. Half-assed eye contact,
The surge of idiotic hope, distant strains
Of ecstatic arias squealed by feeble brains,
The sense that one's shoes might be mistracked,
As Heaven sweetly beckons teasingly.
And there stands Juliet, *ta da*, entranced,
Ready for Paradise, after you have danced,
And spoken magic words so new and free.
And then your cell phone honks out "Running Bear,"
And someone yells "The cops have towed your car!"
And thunder blasts, and you're left where you are,
With desperate dreams expiring everywhere.
Then you need a sympathetic song
To pick you up to barely limp along.

68]
Sweet Rage in Athens

If you thought breaking that mask
Was all you needed to do
And that relocation would erase everything
You were almost right. Almost.
Because nothing erases everything.

Not that it always matters
Or that always mattering always matters
Or that we don't sort of live by erasures
One hopes will do the job.

It's like music, right? So what you hear
In well-timed silence always does matter
When you are listening hard enough—
Or at least well enough.

I do agree about that mask, though,
Even if it was a fine piece of work.
How you had hovered over it!
Thinking of Santorini,
The island of explosion.

69]
Friends, Romans, No Fault, No Foul

Cicero's glee about Caesar's fall
Sprang from ideas about tyranny,
And Brutus looked heroic, briefly,
Till things fell apart, as things will fall,
And the crew of envious or of dreaming men
Murdered that great state's great dignity
And doomed themselves remorselessly
As Anthony's force destroyed them then.
These ideas you have, let me observe,
Have consequences you may not foresee,
But I do not think you wish to hear from me
Questioning of your mind or of your nerve.
One goes one's way and only understands
At last what happened to Cicero's bloody hands.

70]
To Charon, Preparing To Cross the Río Bravo

I hope that thing is solider than it looks.
I'd hate to drown here on my way to Hell,
But if I *have* to sink, I might as well,
And, who can tell from all the dusty books
What happens when a poet doubly croaks?
It may be like a magic double negative
That cancels out damnation, lets me live
In Paradise with all the decent folks
Whose virtues overrode their petty sins
And let them glide above the infernal smoke
That fills the valley where the sinners choke.
Behold their spotless robes and nasty grins.
Wait a minute, Charon, my apologies,
But I am swimming. See you in Hades.

71]
Centrifugal Relationships

Centrifugal relationships work for the young.
Their volatile vigor leaves the heart untapped
And the merry music both unsung and sung,
When all is over, the half-full bottles capped,
Plays in memory without elegiac tones.
These are the stuff of emotional scenes,
Of laughter, parties, comic shouts and groans:
For youth, these embody what life means.
Later, perhaps, that centrifugal force
Becomes the plague of human happiness
As the Odyssean mind's homeward course
To spouse and hearth diminishes restlessness.
The weary traveler arrives to cool his heels
To find disorder, crazily spinning wheels.

72]
The Cosmic Aztec Bribe System

Cuauhtemoc crossed the river; his hopes were high,
And how his prospects glittered in the sun,
As he organized his wishes and said good-bye
To all the pyramids of gold he had won!
"No friction, no traction," he said quietly,
"No conflict, no action," and, when he had found
A place he could defend easily,
He built cash connections with everyone around.
And when the moon shot down a storm of rays
To poison this king, and Orion frowned,
And gravity tweaked and twisted the earth for days,
The chief hummed along with that ferocious sound,
And sometimes rose and danced now and then,
And sang "No friction, no traction" once again.

73]
Pegasus in a Squeeze Chute

Some efflorescence is inevitable,
Despite the diamond's cold integrity,
And one can still be fairly comfortable
Despite embarrassing anxiety.
This Nueces strip of desperation,
Somewhere between Hell and Helicon,
Is no place for a final conversation
Or anything else to meditate upon.
Let it ride, then, I say, if it rides:
And let things develop however they will
In whatever time time slowly provides
Until some time when we have time to kill
Analyzing anecdotes memory compiled
Of wasted time and foolishness run wild.

74]
The Air Parade of Pelicans

If the mind whips left and down before the breeze
Like a gull just where the chorusing breakers course
And beaks its prey and looks around to seize
More vivid nutriment, alacrity and force,
Agility and quickness, in instant conjunction,
Satisfy its purpose, its dynamic correctness,
And the surging rhythm of its essential function
Imposes an authoritative gestural directness.
Yet the parade of pelicans, each dignified,
Like Chaucer's procession of lonely, bardic souls,
Attuned diversely to the schedule of the tide,
Exults in the gliding perfection it controls.
And this melancholy loneliness of mind
Leaves consolation flapping behind.

75]
The General Direction of the Minimal

The name of the play was *Don't Say You're Here
When You're Not All There*, and it starred, I believe,
Lillian Fish, King Kong, and Lassie, that year
Drawing raves, if memory serves to deceive,
But we didn't go—there was something about a hat
Or a color, and then World War Three arrived
To gray our hair just weathering all that,
But though that tempest bellowed, we survived,
And now we stand in line again to see
The same play, this time with Lash LaRue,
A washed-up whale, and Captain Kangaroo,
Newly-dealt ghosts, clear cards where we
Read past and future as though the present cared
Or the future knew, or the past had dared.

76]
Back to *Ad Fontes* Again

If a bird's voice proclaims he is not there
And gravity denies its appetite,
And grammar itself shrugs, law does not care,
And madness has gone to sleep, why fight
Unless the very friction of conflict
Provides a reason to contradict?
The angels of the universe conceal,
With subtle motions of their blessed wings,
The cursed truth, whose logical appeal
Defaces and distorts all valued things.
Though John the Baptist headed off the rise
Of misbegotten insight, cogent lies,
Across the Jordan still come countless tribes
Of envy-driven scholars, horn-tooting scribes.

77]
Sam the Sham Blows Away the National Anthem

"One, two, three, *cuatro*..."

We had Martin Heidegger lined up for this,
But he died, if that's the right word, and after that
Nobody volunteered for a long time,
But somebody had a ten-tequila dream,
And there was the man, rockin' San Antone,
The actual capital of our nation,
And he kind of drug us out of the slop,
And lifted us up, screaming and prancing,
And even the redneck brothers were dancing.

78]
Ten Bucks Says I Can Assassinate Emotion

And once we have formalized informality,
We blithely go from there to designate
Ignorance potential, chaos variety,
And insufficient earliness replaces "too late."
Forgive a certain recalcitrance of mind
In this, too much fresh dust has choked
My vocabulary, and all the words I find
Fit nowhere in the text invoked.
Let me walk outside in the garden awhile until
The fit passes, and, if I then return,
It may be that compromise will
Turn out less impossible to learn.
As Swinburne asks in one exotic verse,
"What new sweet thing would love not relish worse?"

79]
The Ballad of Too Many Mariachis

Like the sands of many oceans,
Ordered by raging harmony,
They stand before my bloodshot eyes
And play on endlessly.

Roosters crow, church bells ring,
Sirens scream, but this harmony
Insists it will assimilate all,
And play on raucously.

I fiddle with the burlap mask,
And the dead count off painfully,
And pray for cooler tombs than this,
Beyond betrayal finally.

Being divested of rank flesh,
So they claim, again and again,
Leaves the spirit cool and fresh,
Much happier than when locked in.

Never take the word of the dead
When they disparage living,
Or that of weeping demons, man,
Who say they need forgiving.

80]
Besworn, Bemused

Giving the wind a good talking to,
I forge the convolutions of regret,
And its discomfortable companions renew
Their duty with quibble, stitch, and fret
To pass the night busily, whatever I do,
Murmuring of treachery, dishonor, and debt,
Whispering suspiciously that nothing is true,
And nothing has happened worth remembering yet.
Yet I defy the scissors of detraction
And endorse my own form of withering scorn
For both regret and forged retraction
To swear myself now unforsworn.
Thus doubly I preserve that former oath:
I renew it now, and I regret it, both.

81]
A Guide to Literary Study

> "No use telling you much about that."
> —*Heart of Darkness*

You don't have to believe in sophistry
To be literate; you don't have to fake
As do the professionals, who always take
The path of superficiality;
You need not glibly find in Hemingway
The latest horrors of insensitivity,
Or hormones in Homer, who could not see
Pedagogy's chariot dashing his way.
Don't scatter silly terms around to show
How truly free from prejudice you are,
How Freud and Marx, a densely double star,
Light up so well what seems to be below.
Wise words bounce off thick skulls, but these
May shield you from the fate of Thersites.

82]
Psalm and Surgery

I have seen the wicked in power, spreading
Himself like a green bay tree, so said
The Psalmist, who never thought that, years ahead,
Autumn winds would have his virtues shedding.
The verb "to ghost," as when a waif of mist
Ghosts into some distant Northern bay,
Describes how hope will smile and steal away
As the baffled bully shakes his empty fist.
His last word, "Nothing," wraps his memory
In mocking silence, while his parasites,
Squealing for their imaginary rights,
Divide his brutal treasures enviously.
I reach for a pen as for a deadly knife,
Inscribing a true record of a scoundrel's life.

83]
Cleghorn Resists the Various Swirls of Evil

The preposition shudders politely when
A cutthroat solipsist invites it in,
And shyly declines his invitations
To join his murdered nominalizations,
His cold, intransitive redundancies
Pickled in glass, words that neither please
Nor move, motionless as the center of pain
In a sinking island sunk in a hurricane.
"Why, sir," she whispers, "I didn't mean to win,
But ever since William of Normandy came in
I've gathered force, and, alas, your frantic dream
To drown the world in a fantastic stream
Has withered, and you are no longer strong.
Believe me, sir, follow the lemmings along."

So wrote Mr. Cleghorn, and saved his text
And closed his laptop, frowning a bit,
For greater labor awaited him next
And he was not yet composed for it.
Against his personal code of action,
He had slept in a red shirt, carelessly,
And he felt that invidious subtraction
Of force that accompanies inevitably
Such disregard for cosmic propriety
And leads to poor judgment both in poetry
And in the war of life, where certainly
Color sucks away sensitivity.
Dressed as clowns, thus, in Morpheus' arms,
Sleeping fools multiply their harms.

And foolishness here is a rich resource,
He thought, reflecting on the bureaucrats
Who seek to keep the city down by force,
Predatory gangsters, scheming rats,
Networked against pressure from outside
To recognize justice and the Constitution,
To give up conspiracy, xenophobic pride,

Blackmail, bribery, theft, and pollution,
To exile the chiseler, the fake, and the buffoon
Who manufacture credentials from trash,
Grease the right palms (thank you, cousin!), and soon
Convert these shameless forgeries to cash
And smirk to think how the honest man's labor
Buys electricity for his well-connected neighbor.

Growling bloodthirstily, three deadly wolves appear,
Greeting their master, emerging from his fit,
Three whom Cerberus would flee in fear,
Dire wolves indeed, as ever biscuit bit,
And Cleghorn calls all three ferocious creatures
And hauls them by the ears and roughly pets
Their shaggy coats, examining their features,
Claws, and fangs, and as each wolf gets
His morning greeting, he comfortably reposes
Himself in a strategic, warlike position
From which, no doubt, he fiercely proposes
To tear and mangle all opposition.
Thus, surrounded by three mighty dogs from Hell,
Their master meditates and speaks a secret spell.

Barricaded in eccentricity
Of a kind, alert to angel whisperings
And curious voices fluting delicately
Essences of many marvelous things,
He reaches toward a lost integrity
And hears the ghosts of long-lost harmony.

84]
Meeting in Green Light

In that parade of corpses, one turned
To look at me. The green moonlight
Scorched her cadaverous face and burned
It greenish pale and deathly white.
Green fangs smirked familiarity,
And a sudden spark lit up one dead eye
As she hoarsely crooned, "Hey, babe, it's me.
You used to say speed kills. That's still a lie.
What kills you, fast or slow, is that you die."
Cold inside, but this wrecked specter
Awakening some sad sympathy yet,
I croaked out in a stunned response to her:
"The alleyways and dungeons I forget,
For angels of sunlight dragged me out
And wrapped me with jasmine and morning glory,
And sweet dreams shifted my mind about,
To sacred miracles in a marvelous story.
They gave me cool white wine and cantaloupe
And pride was driven out by mindless hope."
"So dogs do yap and howl in Heaven, then,"
She said and stared vindictively at me,
"Just as they do for burning devils when
The cold moon shines upon the murderous sea."
"Perhaps," I said, "but words one understands
Are ruled by a magic kept out of our hands,
And whippoorwills' disturbing song at night
Fades out as nighthawks launch themselves for flight."

85]
Driving Slowly Past the Do Buzz Inn

What I thought was a flash of amorous grace
Must have been something else that happened there,
And now I try to shape a kind of prayer
For absolution, for it was in that place
I took a sign one way, and, with a piety
Seeming wise, engaged it for foundation
Of days of deep devoted meditation,
Arriving in this numb absurdity.
O Venus, naughty daughter of sweet, dark night,
I blame thee not, for thy reverence
Makes many a bull to jump the barbed-wire fence,
And, anyway, my brain is rarely right.
Let me just fake regret and quickly go,
With wisdom, now, I never sought to know.

86]
Harry Crews Walks at Midnight, Slapping Yellow Flies

No point thinking much about the pay.
It's counterfeit, son, and all it ever buys
Is trouble you don't need. Surprise, surprise.
No one needs that stupid bullshit anyway.
First thing a writer should do if he wants to write
Is to eat one ton of grits, and not one ounce
Less, load a pulpwood truck, get drunk, and pounce
On that typewriter and hammer the thing all night.
Do this a thousand times, take your masterpiece
To your girlfriend's house, lay it by the door,
Set fire to it, and, as the flames begin to roar,
Holler, "Hallelujah! Call the police!"
This is step one. Next time I'll take you through
Some of the easier details of step two.

87]
Hydrology of Reconciliation

The river has backed up into the arroyos where
Now kingfishers watch and strafe the fish.
The reservoir upstream was full; there
Had to be a release of water. I wish
All our dilemmas were solved so fluently.
The water finds its level, extends its grace
To thirsty land, coasting toward the sea,
Dispensing old rain to each adjacent place.
When part of the mind is about to overflow
And part is suffering psychic dehydration
One needs that overcharge to freely go
Downstream to bring refreshment, restoration,
So all will prosper, heal, and gladly grow.
Time helps us to regulate the flow
That regulates what happiness we know.

88]
No Mr. Kurtz

Clusters of vacuums rove through time,
Their drift a menace of poison and spite,
Savaging goodwill's salvational light,
Replacing wisdom with damage and crime.
Are you there, saints? Speak up, Socrates!
I'm cursing the day all loveliness was born:
This octopus has me writhing on my knees,
Surrendering to evil, dementedly forlorn,
Somebody in heaven, with your blessed mouth,
Holler out the password, the magical code,
Preventing my shabby ass from going south
With a vicious mind on a hell-bound road.
"All I want is justice," Conrad's white man said;
Give me redemption protecting me instead.

89]
The Recovery of Oswald Alving

He woke: "My paints, Mother, for suddenly
I see in your countenance a subject for
A masterpiece neither an illness nor
Inky artificiality
Can block from the sustaining light of day.
I've dreamed of healing tragicomedy
And learned to dream my author's dreams away.
If you will kindly sit and look at me
In the morning light, I'll put luminosity
On canvas, all indifferent things aside,
To generate your violent sympathy
And fix emotion's vast and swirling tide.
The spirit is upon me, now, and I'll
Swiftly paint that devastated smile."

Acknowledgments

The following poems, some of them now revised, were previously published as noted below. My thanks to the respective editors for their kind consideration.

DREICH 7 (Scotland), April 2021, "Drama Critic Dismasted by *Gone with the Wind*."

The Lit Quarterly (Canada), Spring 2021, "The Sophist Counts His Chickens."

Harbinger Asylum, Winter 2019, "Upon this Rock."

Parhelion, October 2019 "Regeneration of Love," "Run Them Chickens Out of the Circles of Purgatory," "Sweet Rage in Athens," "The Wobbly Pendulum Threatens to Strike."

Ashvamegh (India), February 15, 2016, "Hawk in the Mist."

The Write Place at the Right Time, January 22, 2016 (Winter/Spring). "The Line of Pelicans," now titled "Air Parade of Pelicans."

Sonder (UK), October 8, 2015, "A Little Ham for the Kaiser."

The Sonnet Scroll, October 6, 2015, "Ominous Sounds from the Getty Hexameters," "Cold Water Wisdom Up North," "Colonel Sanders Needs Love, Too."

The Corvus Review, October 1, 2015, "Valediction from the Train West," "The Owl Soliloquizes a Ghostly Good-Bye."

Life and Legends 3, June 30, 2015, "The Incredible Recovery of Oswald Alving."

Synesthesia Literary Journal, 3.1, March 30, 2015, "The Wrong End of I-35"; September 4, 2015, "Balaam's Burrito on the Act of Treason"; "Jack Ruby's Smoked Ribs Recipe"; October 23, 2014, "The Slayer of Pain."

Boston Poetry Magazine, August 5, 2013, "The Cosmic Aztec Bribe System."

The Bicycle Review, June 16, 2013, "Meeting in Green Light."

The Dead Mule School of Southern Literature, February 2013, "Harry Crews Walks at Midnight, Slapping Yellow Flies."

Anastomoo (Australia), May 25, 2012, "Ad Fontes Again."

Lucayos (The Bahamas), January 10, 2011, "Hydrology of Reconciliation."

Lucid Rhythms, July 2010, "Centrifugal Relationships."

Willows Wept Review, June 2, 2010, "Meditation in a Mild Hurricane."

Poetry Life & Times (UK), various dates, "The Best Tlacoyos in Chickasawhatchee," "Downtown Waco. Midnight. Heidegger Looks at the Moon," "The Recirculation of the Minimal," "The Swarm."

R. W. Haynes, Professor of English at Texas A&M International University, has published poetry in many journals in the United States and in other countries. As an academic scholar, he specializes in British Renaissance literature, and he has also taught extensively in such areas as medieval thought, Southern literature, classical poetry, and writing. Since 1992, he has offered regular graduate and undergraduate courses in Shakespeare, as well as seminars in Ibsen, Chaucer, Spenser, rhetoric, and other topics. In 2004, Haynes met Texas playwright/screenwriter Horton Foote and has since become a leading scholar of that author's remarkable *oeuvre,* publishing a book on Foote's plays in 2010 and editing a collection of essays on his works in 2016. Haynes also writes plays and fiction. In 2016, he received the SCMLA Poetry Award ($500) at the South Central Modern Language Association Conference. In 2019, two collections of his poetry were published, *Laredo Light* (Cyberwit) and *Let the Whales Escape* (Finishing Line Press).

www.ingramcontent.com/pod-product-compliance
Lightning Source LLC
Chambersburg PA
CBHW021150090426
42740CB00008B/1031